I0804592

PIANO Praise & Worship

Volume #3

Creative Piano Settings by FRED BOCK

TABLE OF CONTENTS

CHANGE MY HEART, O GOD 34
HE WHO BEGAN A GOOD WORK IN YOU 17
HOW BEAUTIFUL 2
I LOVE THE LORD 20
IT'S A HAPPY DAY (And I Thank God For the Weather) . 31
LET THERE BE PRAISE! 6
LORD, I LIFT YOUR NAME ON HIGH 28
THE LORD IS MY LIGHT 38
MY DESIRE 22
SPIRIT SONG 14
THERE IS A REDEEMER 24
THY WORD 9
WE ARE AN OFFERING 12

All of these selections are brand new arrangements by Fred Bock and do not appear in any other piano collection. Might we suggest you take a look at these additional *Praise & Worship* arrangements by Fred Bock contained in Volumes 1 and 2 of this series.

Piano Praise & Worship #1 (BG0749)

FATHER, I ADORE YOU • GIVE THANKS • GLORIFY THY NAME • HE IS EXALTED • HIS NAME IS WONDERFUL • HOW MAJESTIC IS YOUR NAME • I LOVE YOU, LORD • MAJESTY • OH HOW HE LOVES YOU AND ME • OUR GOD REIGNS • SEEK YE FIRST THE KINGDOM OF GOD • SING HALLELUJAH TO THE LORD • THOU ART WORTHY • WE BRING THE SACRIFICE OF PRAISE • WE WILL GLORIFY

Piano Praise & Worship #2 (BG0788)

ALL HAIL, KING JESUS • AS THE DEER • AWESOME GOD • EMMANUEL • HE HAS MADE ME GLAD • I EXALT THEE • I WILL CALL UPON THE LORD • JESUS, NAME ABOVE ALL NAMES • LORD, BE GLORIFIED • OPEN OUR EYES • PRAISE THE NAME OF JESUS • SANCTUARY • SHINE, JESUS, SHINE • THIS IS THE DAY

Fred Bock Music Company

HOW BEAUTIFUL

Twila Paris
Arranged by Fred Bock

Warmly and tenderly

mf
ten.
mp
ten.

Like a hymn-Legato
ten.
mf
ten.
mf
brighter tempo

accelerando
broaden
mp
a tempo
rit.
mp
8va
p
p

LET THERE BE PRAISE!

Melodie and Dick Tunney
Arranged by Fred Bock

Brightly, with rhythmic drive

Lightly
mp
rit.
a tempo
mf
mp
f
mp (echo)
mf
no ritard.
f

ff
mp
mf
f
f
f
subito p
mf
f
subito p
slight accelerando
Broaden
ff
r.h.

THY WORD

Amy Grant & Michael W. Smith
Arranged by Fred Bock

Moderato

mf
mf
f
subito mp

Stately
f
broaden
mp
p

WE ARE AN OFFERING

Dwight Liles
Arranged by Fred Bock

Worshipfully, with feeling

3
mp
mf
8va
mf

SPIRIT SONG

John Wimber
Arranged by Fred Bock

Moderato, with conviction

f
mf
f
mp

rit.
a tempo
rit.

HE WHO BEGAN A GOOD WORK

Jon Mohr
Arranged by Fred Bock

Brightly, with light rhythmic drive

mf
mf

f
mp
f
rit.
ff
ped.

I LOVE THE LORD

Richard Smallwood
Arranged by Fred Bock

Warmly

r.h.
mf
8va
f
mf
mf
f
mf
mp
8va

MY DESIRE

Lillian Plankenhorn
Arranged by Fred Bock

Meditatively

* "Jesus, the Very Thought of Thee" (John B. Dykes)

Optional: start here

mf
ped.
f
mf
ten.
ten.
mp
p
pp

THERE IS A REDEEMER

Melody Green
Arranged by Fred Bock

Warmly and smoothly

mf
legato
stronger
mp
mf

f
mf

Broaden
f
ten. ten.
mp
ten. ten.
mf
f
rit.
ped.

LORD, I LIFT YOUR NAME ON HIGH

Rick Founds
Arranged by Fred Bock

Moderato, with rhythmic drive

f
mf
f
ff

f
broaden
ff
8va

IT'S A HAPPY DAY
(And I Thank God For The Weather)

Gary Pfeiffer
Arranged by Fred Bock

Joyfully, with a triplet "feel"

legato
a tempo
f
slightly slower, more relaxed
ff

subito mp
mf
f
p
slower, in triplet feel
f
ten.
ten.
ten.
a tempo
8va
8va

CHANGE MY HEART, O GOD

Eddie Espinosa
Arranged by Fred Bock

Brightly, with a mariachi-band flavor

3
f
3
3
f
3
Like the beginning
no ped.
ped.
simile

r.h.
f
r.h.
ped.
r.h.
3
f
3
3
f
3

8va(both hands)
[f]
mp
ff
mf
Like the beginning
no ped.
ped.
no ped. simile
f
mf broaden

THE LORD IS MY LIGHT

Pauline Michael Mills
Arranged by Fred Bock

Rhythmically

mf
mp
mf

slight rit.